Flying Disks

Sharon Callen

A disk is a toy that you throw in the air to make it fly.

It's a Fact

Children have played with flying disks for more than 70 years.

Flying disks are made of plastic.

You can use a plastic plate to make your own flying disk.

It's a Fact

There are more than 20 flying disk games that you can play.

Disks are fun to throw to your friends.

They can try to catch them.

It's a Fact

Dogs like to catch disks too!

You can learn to throw a disk.

What To Do

1. Stand in an open space.

2 Hold the top of the disk with your thumb.

3 Rest your pointer finger on the rim of the disk.

4 Hold the bottom of the disk with your other three fingers.

5 Turn your body to face where you are going to throw the disk.

6 Bring the disk to your chest.

7 Throw the disk.

You can make a disk fly!